Original title:
Verdant Verses

Copyright © 2025 Creative Arts Management OÜ
All rights reserved.

Author: Colin Leclair
ISBN HARDBACK: 978-1-80566-632-5
ISBN PAPERBACK: 978-1-80566-917-3

Footprints in Foliage

In the woods, oh what a sight,
Green leaves dance in morning light.
A squirrel leaps with a loud smack,
While I trip over an old knapsack.

A rabbit giggles, oh what a prank,
Drawing doodles in the swampy dank.
I try to sketch, it looks like stew,
Next to a tree, where the frog says, "Boo!"

Mushrooms wiggle in the breeze,
They're plotting tricks with stealthy ease.
I roast marshmallows on a log,
While a hedgehog steals my croaking frog.

Breezy laughter fills the glade,
As I receive a mossy upgrade.
My shoes are green, my socks a mess,
In the forest, fashion's just a guess!

The Language of Chlorophyll

In a garden, plants all chat,
Their gossip's loud, like cats that spat.
"Did you see the squirrel's silly dance?"
"Oh, I did! It's like he's in a trance!"

Leaves wiggle, trying to make a point,
"I swear the bees have formed a joint!"
"And those tomatoes think they're cool,"
"But they're just squishy in the pool!"

Petals in the Breeze

Petals laugh as they float away,
Blowing kisses to the sunlit day.
"Catch me if you can!" they tease,
While dandelions sneak like they're on skis.

Butterflies giggle with cotton candy wings,
"Can you hear the froggies sing?"
" Croak, croak, ribbit!" they croon,
Making symphonies with the afternoon!

Vibrant Roots

Roots underground plot a wild spree,
"Push up a daisy and shout, 'Look at me!'"
Worms are the bouncers, bouncing about,
"No weeds allowed, don't scream or shout!"

A radish whispers, "I'm too cool to sprout,"
While carrots giggle, wiggling out.
"Let's throw a party down here tonight!"
And the tubers chant, "Oh what a sight!"

Soliloquy of Ferns

Ferns gather, sharing their leafy woes,
"Why do humans walk on their toes?"
"I'd rather be grounded, not floating high!"
As the breeze tickles, all ferns reply.

A wise old fern declares in jest,
"Let's hold a meeting and put it to rest!"
"We'll form a club and wear ferns as hats,"
"With all handsome fronds and no silly chitchats!"

Canopy of Dreams

Under leaves that wave and sway,
Squirrels plot their grand ballet.
A branch breaks free, a nut's farewell,
Nature's circus, all is well!

Frogs in tuxedos leap and play,
Toads provide the DJ's sway.
With every jump, a comedy,
In this green-tinted symphony!

Sylvan Serenades

Owls hoot jokes in moonlight's gleam,
Goldfinches perform on a sunny beam.
Dancing flowers, tangle their roots,
Grass tickles toes, no time for boots!

Bees don hats, sipping sweet tea,
A picnic spread for all to see.
Ants bring snacks, with a joke or two,
In this woodland, laughter renews!

Leafy Echoes

Whispers in the breeze, so sly,
Trees gossip, "Did you see that fly?"
Branches creak with laughter loud,
A breeze becomes a playful cloud!

Bugs in shades enjoy the sun,
Claiming nature's all in fun.
With every rustle a chuckle flows,
Among the foliage, humor grows!

Green Canvases

Painting laughs with every stroke,
Mossy rocks, beneath a cloak.
Hummingbirds play peek-a-boo,
While daisies prance, "Come join the crew!"

Artful roots twist and bend,
As playful pixies take a trend.
Crafting smiles in every nook,
Nature's canvas—come take a look!

Harmony of the Hollow

In a hollow where the big frogs croak,
Raccoons dance and the owls choke.
They juggle acorns, what a sight,
Under the moon, they party all night.

Squirrels play banjo, the chipmunks cheer,
As a wise old turtle brings up the beer.
The fireflies twinkle, join in the fun,
Making mischief till the morning sun.

A raccoon wearing a tiny hat,
Tells a joke about a silly cat.
Trees sway gently, laughing out loud,
As nature's quirks draw a merry crowd.

A gathering where all are clowns,
Beneath the leafy, playful crowns.
With buzzing bees as their DJ crew,
In the hollow, the fun is always anew.

Unveiling the Underbrush

In the underbrush where critters meet,
A family of rabbits dance on their feet.
With a wiggle and hop, they challenge a squirrel,
Who rolls his eyes in a furry whirl.

A hedgehog thinks he can join the race,
But spikes and speed, what a silly place!
The bush might shake with their laughter loud,
As they frolic in chaos, nature's proud.

Mice play tag with a dandelion puff,
While the grumpy old toad says that's enough!
But up comes a snail with a 'slow and steady',
Determined to win with no need for speed, he's ready.

The underbrush hides a carnival spree,
With fairies giggling, what fun to see!
Each leaf a stage, each shadow a dream,
In this playful realm, nothing's as it seems.

Trellis of Dreams

Climbing vines weave a story so bright,
With tomatoes gossiping day and night.
The carrots argue about who's the best,
While peas perform in a fancy dress.

Under the sun, they laugh and grow,
A world of whimsy, with tomatoes like snow.
Beans swing high in a gentle breeze,
And caterpillars join them, doing the twist with ease.

It's a garden party with veggies galore,
Where radishes dance with a root vegetable encore.
Past the fence, the old cat naps away,
While the plants tell jokes and bask in the day.

In this trellis of dreams, all things collide,
Where fruit and fun get joyously tied.
With laughter and colors, what a delight,
Nature's fabric creating pure delight.

Heartbeats of the Biosphere

The biosphere hums a cheerful tune,
With frogs croaking softly to the glowing moon.
A dance floor created from moss and leaf,
Where beetles strut with style and belief.

Bunny bops with a pop and a hop,
While a curious fox takes a break to stop.
In this vibrant world, they share their dreams,
As consciousness ripples through flowing streams.

A wise old owl with spectacles peeks,
Exchanging winks with the sly little squeaks.
Each heartbeat syncs like a whimsical song,
In the biosphere's embrace, nothing feels wrong.

Laughter echoes through the lush green expanse,
With every creature joining the dance.
It's a party of life, wild and free,
A heartbeat symphony, come dance with me!

Blossoming Thoughts

In the garden of silly dreams,
Where daisies wear polka dots,
A dandelion sings loud and clear,
While butterflies play hopscotch spots.

The carrots hold a dance-off,
As radishes pipe up with song,
A cabbage leads the conga line,
While peas just can't help but pong.

The roses blush in laughter bright,
As tulips twirl in fleeting flight,
In petals soft, they giggle high,
Underneath the sunlit sky.

So come and romp among the blooms,
With nature's quirks, we face our doom,
For in this patch of joyous weeds,
Humor grows from playful seeds.

The Grove's Tender Secrets

In a grove where whispers grow,
Trees gossip of great delight,
An oak tells tales of squirrel slips,
While pinecones fall in muffled fright.

The saplings share their silly woes,
About shadows and sun's warm glare,
But who peeks through the leafy veil?
A raccoon with mischief to spare.

Fungi wear their colorful hats,
While moss does its best to pose,
The breeze sends giggles through the leaves,
As laughter dances in prose.

So venture forth and hear their tales,
For nature's humor never fails,
In this grove of merry cheer,
Joy and laughter draw us near.

Emerald Whispers

In fields of green where laughter plays,
The blades of grass make funny jokes,
While daisies tease the sleepy bee,
And kittens chase elusive smokes.

A frog in shades croaks serenades,
As crickets join in on the fun,
They tap dance in the evening light,
Making mischief 'til the night's done.

The trees are swaying, feeling spry,
With branches waving side to side,
And in their shade, a picnic waits,
With sandwiches that giggle wide.

So join the laughter in this space,
Where greens are full of sly embrace,
Emerald whispers fill the air,
As nature smiles with playful flair.

Lush Melodies of Spring

In springtime's grasp, the pranks unfold,
With flowers posing—who's the best?
A tulip claims a royal crown,
While violets jest and have a jest.

The bumblebees buzz in a tune,
Dancing round with hops and skips,
They bring back news from flower tribes,
And share their latest honey tips.

A worm recites a limerick,
As raindrops sway to the sweet beat,
While ladybugs roll in the grass,
And butterflies fly with pattering feet.

So let us sing in blossoms bright,
About the fun in morning light,
For springtime's humor, soft and sweet,
Brings joy to every heart it meets.

Petals in the Breeze

Petals dance and whirl with glee,
Caught in playful winds, carefree.
A bee buzzes by, quite the charmer,
Thinking he's a floral farmer.

A leaf fell down and hit my head,
'Twas nature's joke from up ahead.
I laughed so hard, it made me sneeze,
Now I'm allergic to the trees!

The grass grows tall, it starts to sway,
Waving hello like it's ballet.
A squirrel leaps from branch to branch,
In its nutty mind, it does a dance.

So let's all join this leafy spree,
And dance around, wild as can be.
With petals soft and laughter free,
Nature's stage is our decree.

Sunlit Sonnet

The sun peeks out, a grin on high,
With beams that tease, they light the sky.
I squint my eyes and shield my face,
As shadows play a silly chase.

A lizard sunbathes on a stone,
Worms wiggle past, all on their own.
I trip, I fall, and then I yell,
They give a wink, all is quite well!

The daisies giggle in a row,
Their petals bright, a sunny show.
I swear they winked when I walked by,
Caught in their bloom, I can't deny.

So let's applaud this sunny stage,
Where nature's humor steals the page.
With laughter bright, we soak in rays,
In this warm world, let's spend our days.

Underneath the Olive Tree

Beneath the olive, shade so nice,
A picnic spread, let's roll the dice.
The ants parade, all in a line,
Organized chaos, how divine!

A pickle jar, I tried to twist,
But slipped and sent it to the mist.
Olives rolled, a real ballet,
Even they joined in the fray!

The tree just chuckled, leaves a-quiver,
Watching my dance, a gentle shiver.
I bow to nature and to the breeze,
Under the olive, I find my ease.

So let's raise toast to our mishaps bold,
In laughter's warmth, let's not grow old.
With olives ripe and spirits free,
Under this tree, so wittily!

The Green Heartbeat

In gardens lush, the colors pop,
A quirky world that makes me stop.
A gopher peeks, with mischief planned,
Claiming the carrot I just planned!

The daisies chant with laughter bright,
Every flower, a comical sight.
I squint to see a ladybug,
Mocking my dance with a tiny shrug.

The grass tickles my toes with glee,
As I wiggle, wild, so carefree.
The bumblebees join in the fun,
Buzzing along, they've just begun!

So let's embrace this vibrant cheer,
The green heartbeat, loud and clear.
In nature's hands, we are all free,
Together, dancing, you and me!

Nature's Stanzas

In the park I saw a tree,
It waved and said, "Come sit with me!"
A squirrel chattered, full of cheer,
Until a crow swooped down, oh dear!

The flowers danced, they wore bright hats,
To trick the bees, oh those silly brats!
But one bee buzzed, so full of pride,
He got stuck in a rose's side.

A rabbit hopped, all fluffy and white,
Claimed he could outrun the moonlight!
But tripped on a root, fell with a thud,
Got up, shook off, said, "That was just mud!"

The sun set down with a big loud sigh,
Said, "Tomorrow, I'll try to fly high!"
But clouds just laughed, and swirled in glee,
"Let's see you dance, oh bright yellow bee!"

Whispered Secrets of Shade

Under the tree, I heard a joke,
From a chipmunk dressed as a yoke.
He said, "Why can't corn play tricks?
Because it always gets into a fix!"

The leaves giggled, whispering tales,
Of feathered friends with colorful trails.
A robin winked, with a sly little tune,
"Don't trust the owl, he snores by noon!"

The ferns formed a club, quite elite,
With branches crossed, they raised the heat.
But dandelions blew, making a mess,
Said "Join us too, we're the real best!"

In the silence, one ant took a stand,
Declared himself king of the sand!
But when it rained, he quickly fled,
"Next time, I'll stick to my bed!"

Helix of Harmony

Around the pond, frogs croaked in tune,
Singing their hearts out to the moon.
One frog said, "Listen to my bar!"
But he fell in – said, "It's a spa!"

A turtle passed, slow as a snail,
With a cucumber hat, oh what a tale!
He claimed to race, but just sat there,
Said, "Speed is overrated, I swear!"

The fish leaped up, trying to fly,
But hooked itself, said, "Oh my, oh my!"
With a splash and a flop, it danced like a pro,
"Next time, I'll stick to the flow!"

Even the reeds swayed to the beat,
Whispering secrets, oh so sweet.
Said one to another, under the stars,
"Let's party hard, but no more guitars!"

Between the Vines

In the garden, under the vine,
Grapes giggled, "Here, try our wine!"
But one grape gasped, "Not from my side!"
"I prefer juice," it squeaked with pride.

The pumpkin rolled, thinking it's grand,
Said, "I'm a carriage, come take my hand!"
But when it reached the step, oh dear,
It just got stuck, couldn't go near.

The strawberries blushed, all sweet and red,
Gossiped with tomatoes, "What's up ahead?"
They plotted a party, all full of grace,
Until the beets said, "Hey, this is our space!"

But laughter rang out, all mingling sounds,
As everyone joined with leaps and bounds.
Under the stars, with veggies galore,
They danced till the night was no more!

Wilderness Refrain

In the woods a squirrel prances,
Chasing shadows, taking chances.
A raccoon scales a tall pine tree,
Claiming snacks for his next spree.

The owls hoot a silly song,
While the frogs croak all night long.
Nature's laughter fills the air,
A raucous fiesta, with flair!

Beneath the bridge, a fish doth leap,
Splashing life, in joy they sweep.
The bees dance around the flowers,
Taking breaks from their busy hours.

So let's skip, let's whirl around,
In nature's joy, true bliss is found.
With every wiggle, giggle, and cheer,
Life's a party, oh so dear!

The Scent of Moss

A squirrel sneezes, oh the fuss!
Allergies wake him from his bus.
He sniffs the air, then comes the cough,
As mushrooms giggle and shake off.

Pinecones tumble, make a crash,
Frogs leap by in a daring splash.
The mushrooms hold a stinky brew,
'Taste like socks!' says old Matthew.

With each step, the forest grins,
As the hedgehog spins, and spins.
Mossy carpets hold a smell,
'We can't tell if it's good or hell!'

The trees chime in with knock-knock jokes,
While rabbits roll with hooting folks.
In this green maze of laughter found,
Who knew nature could be so sound?

Adaptive Harmonies

The daffodils dance in a row,
With wobbling stems, they steal the show.
The tulips argue, 'I'm the bright!'
While daisies chuckle, taking flight.

A crafty snail with blingy shell,
Moves to jazz, oh what a swell!
Swaying leaves, a tempting tune,
Even worms are getting in the groove!

The tree frogs join with ribbit rhymes,
As ladybugs drum, keeping times.
The butterflies spin in the breeze,
Spreading joy with graceful ease.

In this green scene, all are jesters,
Nature's court, full of masters.
Who knew gardens could chuckle so,
In harmony's glorious show?

Floral Footprints

Upon the trails, flowers grumble,
Their colors shout, while others mumble.
With polka-dot petals, they strut and sway,
While bees slink in, daring to play.

A clumsy dog jumps with cheer,
Trampling blooms without a fear.
They gasp and giggle, 'What a sight!'
Sprouting colors, oh so bright!

The bumblebees orchestrate a band,
Playing tunes on nature's strand.
While ants march in a line so neat,
Carrying snacks for their evening treat.

Laughter echoes through the blooms,
As they embrace their fragrant fumes.
In every petal, joy resides,
In floral footprints, fun abides!

Whispering Woods

In the woods where squirrels scheme,
A raccoon snaps a selfie meme.
The trees all gossip, leaf to leaf,
While birds drop jokes, beyond belief.

A deer walks in with quite a flair,
Sporting antlers like a millionaire.
The owls hoot phrases quite absurd,
As they crack up, no one heard!

Mushrooms laugh behind a tree,
"Hey, did you hear about the bee?
He quit his job, returned to flower,
Said working there was too much power!"

The wind joins in, a breezy tune,
As bushes shimmy, hum a rune.
Each critter plays their part with zest,
In this woodland tale, they jest the best!

Flora's Lull

In the garden, flowers dream,
Daisies giggle, it's a meme.
The roses blush with a sigh,
While tulips wink and pass by.

Bees buzz puns about the sun,
"I'm late for work, oh what a run!"
Each petal flutters, laughing wide,
In this bloom, no need to hide.

Caterpillars throw a dance,
Munching leaves, they seize their chance.
"A worm with glasses? What a sight!
He couldn't see—just took a bite!"

Laughter swirls with fragrant air,
Nature's jesters lead the fair.
Every bloom, each lively shade,
In Flora's world, fun is made!

Echoes in the Meadow

In the meadow, things get wild,
A bunny hops, just like a child.
The daisies clap with silent cheer,
While crickets croon, "We're glad you're here!"

Grasshoppers jump, throw their bets,
On who can dance without regrets.
A sheep joins in with silly glee,
"Count on me for a fun spree!"

The sky is blue, with clouds like cream,
While butterflies chase a silly dream.
"Did you hear?", a flower prattles,
"Bees started a band; they play on rattles!"

With echoes of giggles all around,
In this meadow, joy is found.
Each creature sings in its own key,
Living life, wild and free!

Silhouettes of Nature

At dusk, the shadows start to play,
A fox tells tales of the day.
The owls listen, eyes all wide,
As the moon glows with nature's pride.

The crickets chirp, a nightly show,
With laughs that dance to and fro.
"Why did the crow sit on the wire?"
"Because it was time to retire!"

The trees sway, part of the scene,
Adventuring whispers, crisp and green.
Each silhouette has its own part,
With humor woven in its heart.

As stars twinkle, casting their light,
Nature laughs softly, pure delight.
In the shadows, joy takes flight,
In silhouettes, the world feels right!

Leafy Reveries

In the garden, I found a hat,
Made of leaves and a big old cat.
It purred and danced on the sunny ground,
Sipping dew like it's the best around.

The daisies giggle in the breeze,
As the ants march home with breadcrumbs of cheese.
A butterfly flutters with flair and a twist,
Saying, 'Hey, don't forget me, I exist!'

The gnomes in the yard wear socks that clash,
One's got stripes, the other's a splash.
They gossip and whisper, sharing confessions,
Of secret encounters with local obsessions.

But who knew the grass could be so sly,
Tickling toes as we pass by?
With a hop and a skip, we join the parade,
In the garden of laughter, where none is dismayed.

Garden Pathways

On the path where the daisies play,
A squirrel skates on leaves all day.
He slips and slides with a wink and a grin,
Chasing his shadow, a game to win.

A worm in a bowtie gives a grand speech,
To the cabbage that dreams of being a peach.
"Life in the soil is rather upscale,
With mud masks and flavors that never pale!"

A hedgehog tries hard to dance with style,
But rolls in a ball and sits for a while.
He blushes red like a ripened chick,
And vows to return with some rhythm to pick.

Sunflowers cheer with their heads held high,
As the beetles in tuxedos sway by.
Together they frolic, in quirky delight,
On these garden pathways, everything feels right.

A Symphony of Green

In the grove where giggles bloom,
A frog conducts the choir's zoom.
With bulging eyes and a musical croak,
He waves his arms for the snail to poke.

The crickets strum on rusty strings,
While ladybugs plan their fanciest wings.
With a hop, hop here and a jig, jig there,
They dance like no one has a missing pair!

A behind-the-bush band begins to play,
With uninvited guests that join the fray.
A raccoon tap dances, the fox holds a tune,
The evening blooms bright under a silvered moon.

The leaves ripple laughter, join in the cheer,
The grass invites all for a drink of sweet beer.
With a final wink from the celestial sheen,
They bow to the sounds of their symphony green.

Whispers of Willow

The willow tree pens a poem in the breeze,
With branches that tickle, just like they please.
'Hey, over there, don't stand too close,
You might catch a laugh from a giggling ghost!'

The daisies gossip, with secrets to share,
While vines weave stories in the sun-drenched air.
A chipmunk in glasses recites a lost tale,
Of the time he found grains in a magical pail.

The clouds play peekaboo, with shadows that dance,
As the leaves take turns in a whimsical prance.
All the while, the breeze lets out a sigh,
With whispers of joy drifting up to the sky.

So join in the chorus, find laughter today,
Let the world around you invent a new play.
With fingers entwined in the roots of this thrill,
We'll dance through the whispers of our dear willow's will.

Embrace of the Forest

In the woods, a squirrel danced,
Said to a tree, "You're in a trance!"
Leaves chuckled, swayed with glee,
While a rabbit joined in—oh, so free.

The mushrooms wore their polka dots,
Dancing around in tiny pots.
With every wobble, giggles grew,
Even the ferns shook their heads too.

A bear tried yoga, struck a pose,
Fell on his face—no one knows!
The owls hooted, cracking wise,
While the bunnies rolled their eyes.

In the embrace where laughter's found,
Every creature spins around.
The forest pulses, life in jest,
Who knew nature could be the best?

Sunlit Canopy

Under sun, the bees play tag,
With buzzing laughs, they zig and zag.
A lazy cat napped on a leaf,
Dreaming of fish, what a relief!

Clouds turned into fluffy sheep,
While ladybugs began to leap.
"I can fly!" cried one in pride,
"Just be careful of the ride!"

A sunbeam tickled the frog so bright,
He croaked a tune, what a delight!
Frogs and birds formed a band,
In this wild, whimsical land.

As shadows dance with whispering trees,
Everyone joins in, feeling the breeze.
Sunlit laughter fills the air,
In this joyful, carefree affair!

Hushed Grove Tales

In the grove where shadows play,
The mushrooms gossip every day.
"Did you hear what Owl just said?"
"He's still mad about his bed!"

A turtle wears a fancy hat,
Looks so dapper, what of that?
"I'm off to tea!" he loudly claims,
While passing by the sparrow's games.

The wind, it whispers silly deeds,
"Did you steal my acorn seeds?"
The fox just smirks, with staged surprise,
Underneath those twinkling skies.

Even silence wears a grin,
As creatures play and spin and sin.
In these tales of gentle jest,
Life's a riddle—just be the best!

Meadow Musings

In the meadow, cows play chess,
One moos loudly, just to impress.
Worms wear coats, get fancy too,
While butterflies giggle, fluttering through.

Daisies whisper, sharing secrets,
About the bees—those busy presets.
"Did you see that clumsy ant?"
"Fell right over! He's quite the plant!"

Grasshoppers sing with quirky flair,
Tap dance under the sunlit glare.
A picnic of crumbs shared by the mice,
Surrounded by blooms, oh so nice!

Laughter rings on petals bright,
Nature's fun—what pure delight!
In this meadow, life's a play,
Silly moments brighten the day!

Whispers of Green

In the garden, weeds do dance,
Winking with a cheeky glance.
Plants gossip, they take a chance,
Sipping sunlight, in their trance.

Sassy daisies wear a crown,
While buttercups just flop down.
A rogue snail slips, oh what a clown,
Escaping from a chompy frown.

Rambunctious roots play hide and seek,
While petals giggle, so to speak.
A chubby caterpillar's peak,
In this garden, fun's unique!

With each bloom, the laughter grows,
Tickling toes with gentle throes.
In this patch, silliness glows,
Nature's joy, as everyone knows.

Lush Dreams Awaken

In the meadow, dreams take flight,
Grasshoppers hop with pure delight.
A daisy dressed in morning light,
Prances 'round, a silly sight.

Bumblebees buzz in a choir,
Singing songs of their sweet desire.
While dandelions play with fire,
Blowing wishes, we all conspire.

A snail meanders, takes it slow,
With hair gel made of morning dew.
Slicked back style, quite the show,
Strutting past a blooming row.

Underneath a leafy roof,
Laughter echoes, that's the proof.
In nature's book, we find the truth,
Growing joy, eternal youth!

The Symphony of Leaves

Leaves chatter like old friends,
Sharing gossip as it bends.
Rustling secrets never ends,
Nature's laughter, it transcends.

A squirrel scampers up a tree,
Doing acrobatics, oh so free!
Chasing shadows, filled with glee,
While ants march on, a jubilee.

The flowers bloom, a vibrant show,
Tickled by a passing blow.
Cacti chuckle, tall and slow,
Witty winks from roots below.

Bouncing bunnies hop along,
To a rhythm, nature's song.
In this melody, we belong,
Where smiles bloom and hearts are strong.

Emerald Echoes

In the jungle, laughter roars,
Monkeys swinging, tale galore.
Parrots squawk from leafy shores,
Echoing joy forevermore.

The vines toss jokes from afar,
While flowers giggle, it's bizarre.
In this place, a shining star,
A bouncing frog, a comedy czar.

A curious tortoise winks his eye,
Holding court as time slips by.
Sipping tea, oh my oh my!
With each sip, we all comply.

The grasses sway, tickled by breeze,
Each rustle sounds like cute tease.
In emerald hues, we find the keys,
Unlocking laughter, joy, and ease.

Shadows of Sprouts

In a garden of green, a sprout found a hat,
Wore it with pride, looking quite like a cat.
The sun laughed aloud, its rays all a-glow,
While the daisies danced, putting on quite a show.

A snail rolled by, thinking it quite neat,
Said, "That sprout sure knows how to dress for the heat!"
The sunflower winked, with petals so bright,
"I bet that sprout dreams of partying all night!"

Together in the Thicket

In the thicket so thick, where the wild things play,
A tree limb did joke, 'Just hangin' out all day.'
The bushes giggled, with their leaves all a-flutter,
'What's the deal with roots, they're just in the gutter!'

A raccoon chimed in, munching berries galore,
'This place is a blast! Who could ask for more?'
A rabbit hopped over, quick as a flash,
'Let's throw a bash, come join the cash stash!'

Songs of the Shrubland

In the shrubland sweet, where the critters sing,
A cheeky old crow thought he'd start a fling.
He cawed out a tune, but forgot all the notes,
While the bushes all trembled in their leafy coats.

A fox joined the fun, doing the twist,
Shaking with joy, he couldn't resist.
The flowers cheered loud, in colors so bright,
'This dance is a riot! Let's groove through the night!'

Breath of the Wild

In the breath of the wild, where the air tastes sweet,
A squirrel wore shades, said, 'Oh, isn't life neat?'
He chattered and laughed through the broad leafy lane,
While a hedgehog rolled by, enjoying the gain.

The breeze played a tune, through branches it strolled,
The flowers all giggled, feeling quite bold.
Birds joined the party, with sounds so absurd,
Saying, 'Life's just a song, can you hear every word?'

Gardens of Resilience

In a garden where daisies dance,
Bumblebees wear tiny pants.
The carrots giggle in the sun,
While radishes play tag for fun.

Lettuce whispers silly jokes,
Tomatoes jest with clumsy strokes.
A sunflower shoots a wink so bright,
While peas laugh, 'What a silly sight!'

A rabbit hops with cheeky flair,
Sprouting flowers, unaware.
They twist and twirl without a care,
In this patch of laughter, bright and rare.

Nature's humor thrives, it's true,
Even weeds crack jokes 'bout the dew.
In gardens where laughter reigns supreme,
Life's a funny, leafy dream.

Tangled Roots

Roots that rumble, roots that play,
Tangle up in a comical way.
A potato trips on its own feet,
While turnips guffaw and skip to the beat.

Carrots plot a dance-off show,
With rhubarb cheering, 'Go, go, go!'
But grasshoppers jump, a silly spree,
Leaving tangled roots in pure glee.

Beets get tangled in a leafy kiss,
Claiming it's nature's way of bliss.
They giggle as they wriggle and squirm,
In this soil, all roots can confirm.

So if you find a root that's stuck,
Just laugh it off, that's your luck.
For in this garden of silly fights,
Tangled roots bring the funniest sights.

Soaring Spirits

A butterfly flits with a dash of sass,
While ladybugs gather, wearing glass.
They swirl and circle, all quite merry,
Chasing the wind, not one bit wary.

A frog croaks cheers from the pond,
As dragonflies giggle and grow fond.
"Let's soar," they say, with wings so bright,
And laugh at clouds that drift in flight.

High above, a crow caws loud,
"Join the fun, don't be too proud!"
While sparrows chirp a tune so sweet,
In this sky, every spirit meets.

So let your heart take to the air,
And find the joy waiting up there.
For in this flight of care-free thrills,
Soaring spirits conquer all ills.

Fronds and Fantasies

Fronds wave gently in the breeze,
Whispering secrets like old trees.
A fable spins between the leaves,
Of singing ferns and wishful thieves.

A fox trots by with a feathered hat,
Swearing he's a wizard, fancy that!
With every step, he casts a spell,
On curious critters who listen well.

Squirrels join in, plots they hatch,
To make a tree a perfect patch.
With acorns dancing, they twist and sway,
In this leafy world of wild display.

So gather round, come one, come all,
A frond-filled party, hear the call.
For in this realm of weird fantasy,
Laughter blooms in the tallest tree.

The Art of Wild Blooms

Blooming daisies wear polka dots,
A quirky fashion, they tie knots.
Dandelions blow their puffs with glee,
As tulips laugh, "Come play with me!"

Petunias plan a dance parade,
While violets work on their charade.
Begonias gossip, oh what a sight,
In this flower patch, all feels right.

At night, the moon throws a light show,
Stars twinkle, as blossoms put on a glow.
With fireflies' tunes, they sway and swirl,
Each petal has a story to unfurl.

So in this art of blossoms wild,
Joy springs forth like a happy child.
For every bloom, in colors bright,
Holds laughter within its soft delight.

Meadow Meditations

In fields so green, the grasses dance,
A rabbit hops, seeks a second chance.
The flowers giggle, swaying all day,
"Pick me, pick me!" they shout in play.

The sun shines bright, a sparkling tease,
While bumblebees hum their sweet melodies.
A lazy cow munches with delight,
Saying, "Life's a feast, come join the bite!"

A squirrel buries nuts, oh what a sight,
Claiming, "These snacks will last all night!"
The daisies blush at the joke made,
"Hey, who knew lunch could be this laid!"

As twilight falls, the crickets sing,
Chirping tunes of every silly thing.
The meadow laughs in the fading light,
As dreams of frolic take flight tonight.

Vines of Reflection

In tangled vines, the secrets lie,
A bird retorts, "Don't ask me why!"
The leaves whisper tales of the past,
While squirrels race with such vigor, so fast.

A lazy lizard sips from a pool,
Saying, "Nature's the greatest school!"
The flowers point, giggling in hues,
"Look at that snail; he loves to snooze!"

Vineyards stretch with stories so thick,
A grape rolls by, quick as a tick.
"I'm just a fruit, minding my biz,
But oh, look at those humans do whizz!"

As moonlight casts its silver glow,
Lights dance around, putting on a show.
A party here, no need to pretend,
Nature's laughter will never end.

Sprouts of Hope

Tiny seeds sprout with dreams so grand,
Whispering wishes throughout the land.
A sunflower beams, straight and tall,
"When life gives you shade, just stand, don't fall!"

Earthworms wiggle in joyful cheer,
Singing, "Dirt's our throne; let's make it clear!"
A tiny sprout joins in the fun,
"I may be little, but soon I'll run!"

Ladybugs march in a line, so neat,
Clapping their wings to a rhythmic beat.
"We're on a mission, can't you see?
We've got flight plans for a grand jubilee!"

As day unfolds with sunlight's glow,
Hope fills the air, and laughter will flow.
Every green bud knows just how to cope,
In nature's hands, we find our hope.

Nature's Written Word

Leaves rustle softly, writing in the air,
"Read me! Read me! We have tales to share!"
A wise old tree chuckles with glee,
"My bark's the book; come learn from me!"

The brook bubbles forth with a giggling song,
Saying, "Nature's library is never wrong!"
The stones mumble secrets, beneath their moss,
"We hold history, no need to toss!"

A playful breeze flits and twirls,
Twirling the petals of daffodil girls.
"We've got stories, we share in haste,
Of sunshine dreams that never waste!"

As moonlight dances on pages turned,
Every crickets' chirp is a lesson learned.
Nature's script whispers, beyond just the word,
In endless laughter, our hearts are stirred.

Arborian Euphony

In a forest where trees wear hats,
The squirrels gossip, plotting their chats.
One swings by, quite bold and spry,
Yelling out, "I'm as cool as a pie!"

The owls stay up, to count their sheep,
While the pine trees try to take a leap.
Each branch a dancer, bending with glee,
Chasing shadows, as silly as can be.

Beneath the leaves, a gnome holds court,
Telling tales of a dragon's retort.
With laughter echoing through the space,
They all agree, life's a funny race.

So if you wander, don't be shy,
Join in the fun; give it a try.
For in this glade, the laughter thrives,
Where nature plays, and joy arrives.

Tangles of Time

The vines are tangled, quite a mess,
But what a time to dress up in dress!
A snail waltzed by, tripping on leaves,
Declaring, "Oh, how this laughter weaves!"

A rabbit's stuck in a leafy bind,
While hedgehogs dance, no care in mind.
Time tickles trees, with soft, sweet chimes,
Making even the serious act as clowns at times.

A clock-faced owl hoots, "What's the hour?"
As flowers bloom, showcasing their power.
With petals flapping, like coats on a spree,
They chuckle at the passing bumblebee.

In these wild places, don't look for frowns,
For even the grass seems to wear little crowns.
Laugh along with the flora in sync,
In tangled time, we all need to wink.

Serenity Amongst the Sylva

In the calm of the woods, a bear learned to sing,
Harmonizing with crickets, embracing the spring.
He tripped on a root and fell with a splash,
Moaning, "Next time, I'll stick to a dash!"

The breeze whispered secrets to the tall trees,
With branches swaying, dancing with ease.
A wise old fox slurped acorns like stew,
And said, "It's gourmet; just ask the raccoon!"

Bright fireflies twinkled in a playful parade,
While mushrooms debated the choices they'd made.
Beneath the moonlight, all creatures convene,
Sharing jokes that are fit for a queen.

So settle down in this tranquil domain,
Where even the wind sings a chuckle in vain.
Amongst the greens, in peace we will find,
A giggle that dances through heart and mind.

Wildflower Whimsy

In a patch of wildflowers, the daisies took pride,
Whispering loudly, they never would hide.
A bee joked aloud, "I can't take a break,
This pollen's a party; make no mistake!"

Buttercups giggled, comparing their hues,
While poppies traded their sassy old shoes.
The laughter grew louder with every sunbeam,
As the garden became quite the whimsical dream.

Dandelions daydreamed, blowing their fluff,
Saying, "We're just wishing, but it's never enough!"
With bees in tuxedos, and ants in a line,
The wildflowers boasted, "We're simply divine!"

So frolic in petals, let giggles ensue,
For nature's a stage, and there's room for you.
Join the wildflowers, bring your own cheer,
In this funny bloom, we all gather near.

Patchwork of Greenery

In the garden, weeds take throne,
Dressed like kings on leafy bone.
Lettuce laughs at the spinach stare,
While daisies dance without a care.

Slugs in suits slide on the ground,
Whispering secrets, profound and round.
A patchwork quilt of colors bright,
In this strange, whimsical sunlight.

Cabbages gossip with carrots near,
'Who's your tailor?' they ask with cheer.
The beans are tangled in wild embrace,
As bees buzz out for their high-speed chase.

Potatoes dream of the golden sun,
Claiming each sprout is a special one.
The humor of growth, in greens so bold,
Makes this patchwork a sight to behold.

Threads of Bloom

A sunflower wears shades, looking sassy,
While peonies blush, feeling all classy.
The tulips giggle, they can't contain,
Their impatience for spring's sweet rain.

Bumblebees with tiny tuxedos,
Dance around like connoisseurs of speedos.
Pansies shout, 'Join our grand parade!'
As violets laugh, their jokes well-made.

Dandelions puff like the best of clowns,
Scattering seeds like playful crowns.
In this garden where laughter blooms,
Nature paints with whimsical plumes.

Roses conspire with petals so bold,
Telling stories of love, half-told.
In threads of bloom, there's life and cheer,
Every day in this garden, we steer.

The Verdure Chronicle

Once upon a time in leafy land,
Herbs threw a party, quite unplanned.
Thyme made toasts, with basil in tow,
While parsley twirled in a leafy show.

The cucumbers spoke in whispers sweet,
As carrots jived to the beet's wild beat.
Corn serenaded the nearby beans,
With melodies of summers' dreams.

Radishes blushed from the merry thrill,
While lettuce dared to throw a frill.
This verdant chronicle, a tale so fine,
Of vegetables drinking dandelion wine.

When night fell down, the stars appeared,
Each leafy character, deeply cheered.
And so the garden, in laughter and jest,
Grows stories of joy, which never rest.

Resonance of Roots

Roots underground, having a rave,
Wiggling and jiggling, oh what a wave!
Carrots lead the conga line,
While potatoes groove with a twist of vine.

Old tree trunks whisper tales so far,
Of roots who dreamt of being a star.
They laugh at the flowers' highbrow show,
As the wind hums a soft, silly glow.

Chives shoot jokes that make rocks roll,
While ferns play hopscotch, feeling bold.
In this ground where laughter thrives,
Even the worms are doing high-fives!

Each root and flower, in harmony found,
Creating a symphony deep in the ground.
In the resonance of droll, green delight,
Nature's laughter echoes through the night.

Nature's Lullaby

In the woods a squirrel sings,
While a bear dances on springs.
Birds wear hats made of leaves,
Telling tales that nobody believes.

A frog croaks jokes near a stream,
While ants hustle, a busy team.
The trees giggle in the breeze,
Whispering secrets to the bees.

Clouds puff up with giggles bright,
As sunbeams beam with pure delight.
Nature's laughter, loud and free,
Wraps the world in harmony.

So join the fun, let worries fly,
Dance with the breeze, reach for the sky.
In this lush land where smiles roam,
Every green space feels like home.

Garden of Thoughts

In a patch of soil, thoughts sprout,
Some whisper low, while others shout.
A daisy claims it knows it all,
While roses blush at every call.

The carrots chuckle underground,
As their leafy heads shake around.
Tomatoes compete with a boastful vine,
Saying, "We're the best, come dine!"

A sunflower winks at the moon,
While nightingales hum a funny tune.
In this garden, ideas throng,
Each quirky thought feels like a song.

So plant your dreams within this space,
Watch them grow with a funny face.
In every corner, laughter grows,
As the garden of thoughts merrily glows.

Sprouts of Serenity

Tiny sprouts peek from the ground,
Whispering secrets without a sound.
With each tickle of the sun's warm light,
They sway and dance, what a sight!

Ladybugs wearing polka-dot gowns,
Strut around like little clowns.
Worms do the twist in underground glee,
Throwing a dance party, just wait and see!

Breezes blow with a playful nudge,
As flowers giggle and won't budge.
Here in the calm, silliness reigns,
With nature's laughter echoing through lanes.

So take a stroll through this funny space,
Where joy blooms bold, and troubles erase.
In the garden of peace, don't sulk or pout,
Just laugh with the sprouts and wiggle about!

Flourishing Souls

In a meadow where flowers bloom,
Bumblebees buzz with a hint of gloom.
They've lost their way to the pollen fair,
And now they're circling like they don't care.

Butterflies flutter in silly loops,
Chasing dreams with the grasshopper troops.
Each laugh bursting from petals so bright,
Spreading joy like confetti, what a sight!

The sun grins down with a cheeky wink,
While the moon whispers, "Go on, don't think!"
In this world of silliness grand,
We find solace in nature's hand.

So come and join, let silliness flow,
With flourishing souls, together we grow.
In the arms of this wild, joyous spree,
Life is better, as all can see!

Vibrant Earth

In a garden full of weeds,
A snail plans his escape,
With lettuce on his mind,
He dreams of a grand cape.

The flowers dance in glee,
While frogs sing in a choir,
A bug has lost its way,
Mistaking soil for fire.

The tomatoes wear their hats,
A sunburned shade of red,
They'll be the star of lunch,
And feast on all the bread.

Oh, nature's such a laugh,
With mishaps left and right,
The cucumbers throw a party,
As carrots sneak a bite.

The Lush Concerto

A squirrel plays the piano,
With acorns as his keys,
The birds join in the chorus,
While dancing on the breeze.

The mushrooms form a band,
With toadstools as the drums,
They'll throw a leafy bash,
Inviting all the scums.

The flowers sway and giggle,
As breezes join the tune,
While grasshoppers tap dance,
Beneath the laughing moon.

In this garden concert hall,
Nature's surely a hoot,
With every leaf a laugh,
And every root a boot.

Breezes Through Branches

A breeze tickles the leaves,
Like whispers of the grass,
The trees sway with delight,
In a playful, leafy class.

The branches play tag up high,
With every gust, a game,
The squirrels shout, 'You missed me!'
While branches shake in fame.

Sunlight peeks through the twigs,
Making shadows dance around,
A fox trips on a root,
While twirling on the ground.

With branches swaying low,
On this playground of green,
Nature's a comedy,
With the best cast ever seen.

Dappled Light Chronicles

In the glen where sunlight streams,
The dappled spots do play,
While playful shadows linger,
In an amusing ballet.

A rabbit hops out singing,
With a top hat on his head,
He claims he's quite the dancer,
But trips and lands instead.

The daisies cheer him on,
With petals in a flap,
While butterflies take selfies,
And crickets start to clap.

This tale of light and laughter,
In the woods, a lovely sight,
Where nature spins its stories,
In a world that feels just right.

Growth's Gentle Lullaby

In the garden where gnomes sleep,
The daisies wiggle and beans leap.
Where snails wear hats of shiny gold,
And secrets of nature slowly unfold.

With whispers of leaves in the breeze,
The ants all dance with such ease.
Oh, what a riot, these plants in bloom,
They think they're fine but need a broom!

Toads sing lullabies croaked off key,
While flowers gossip, oh dear me!
The sun rolls out its golden tongue,
In this patch, all's silly and young.

Beneath the soil, worms giggle and grin,
As raindrops puddle, let the fun begin.
Growth's gentle rhythm, a slapstick show,
Nature's jesters put on a glow!

Secrets Beneath the Canopy

Underneath leaves where shadows play,
Squirrels tell tales of yesterday.
With mossy hats and acorn charms,
They trick the mushrooms into their arms.

The robins rehearse a rather loud song,
While woodpeckers tap all day long.
In whispers, the branches reveal a plot,
Of how to annoy the lone parking lot!

Vines twist and twirl, what a sight!
They form a conga line, oh what delight!
The trees exchange jokes, way up on high,
As clouds drift past with a puff and a sigh.

In this leafy maze, every creature prances,
Engaging in laughter as the daylight dances.
Secrets of silliness join in delight,
Beneath the grand canopy, all feels just right!

Moss-Covered Musings

On a stump that's dressed in fuzzy green,
A wise old frog takes up the scene.
He tells of mishaps from long ago,
Like when he mistook a shoe for a toe!

With mossy coats and stylish grace,
The woodland critters gather in place.
A game of charades breaks out by the brook,
While owls pretend to jot down a book.

A squirrel does jazz hands, much to our thrill,
While the river chimes in with a giddy trill.
"Who knew," they all muse with a chuckle and sigh,
That nature's a stage, for those who get high!

In this wild cafe where giggles abound,
The humor of nature knows no bound.
So next time you roam through the forest so wide,
Don't forget to laugh with your mossy guide!

Nature's Poetic Palette

A canvas with colors, bright and bold,
Where flowers and fruits share tales untold.
The bees wear berets, the sun's their stage,
While butterflies flutter like actors in page.

In gardens of laughter, the petals sway,
And tomatoes joke about the kids at play.
With peppers prancing in hues of delight,
Together they stand, oh what a sight!

The trees wear crowns of rustling cheer,
As breezes of laughter tickle the ear.
The daisies deliberate on the best jokes,
While clovers chuckle, feeling like folks.

So here in nature's vivid embrace,
Where humor blooms at a rapid pace.
With each brushstroke, the world finds its glee,
And smiles in clusters, wild and free!

A Tapestry of Chlorophyll

In a leafy world, things get weird,
A squirrel talks back, it's not what we feared.
Gossip of grasses, a ticklish breeze,
The daisy just laughed, fell down on its knees.

The vines have a party, oh what a sight,
They twist and they tangle, all through the night.
A mossy DJ spins tunes from the ground,
While butterflies twirl, no worries abound.

Frogs croak out jokes from their muddy stage,
The worms all chuckle, they're wise for their age.
Then suddenly, petals start throwing confetti,
A bloom said, "I'm hungry, but carrot's too petty!"

With colors so wild, it's a cheerful spree,
Nature in giggles, oh what glee!
The trees make a toast, it's a little absurd,
"To the buds and the blooms, and the laughter we heard!"

Breaths of Earth's Embrace

In the soil's warm hug, a worm sings a tune,
While the daisies dance under the warm afternoon.
"Hey, how's it growing?" a root asks a sprout,
"Pretty good," it replies, "just trying to pout."

The clouds tease the leaves, with a sprinkle of rain,
"Hey, how about sharing, don't be such a pain!"
A robin replies with a chirp full of cheer,
"Don't worry, dear leaves, I'm your sunshine here!"

But the deep forest whispers, "Let's play hide and seek,"
The ferns all giggle, "We won't even peek!"
A bush hides a bunny, it's really quite sly,
While the flowers all blush when the bees buzz by.

With roots intertwined and laughter afloat,
The earth gives a grin, nature's funny note.
In the glow of the twilight, all creatures agree,
Life's all about joy, and the silly we see!

The Language of Ferns

The ferns have a secret, or so they believe,
They gather together, no time to grieve.
Whispering softly, in wavy green tones,
"Did you see that bird? He tried to wear bones!"

A hedgehog beside them is rolling in glee,
"I've got my own spines, but prefer to be free!"
And the mushrooms beside them, they chuckle and glow,
"Now that would be fashion, for a quirky show!"

"What's that up there?" shouts a sprightly young leaf,
"A snail in a shell that's way too brief!"
The others all laugh, in the green meadow low,
"Let's paint him a coat, a grand summer show!"

With laughter and joy, their chatter takes flight,
In the heart of the grove, there's a humorous light.
The earth sways with mirth, what a whimsical turn,
All language in green, while the laughter does burn!

Canopy Harmonies

Up in the canopy, the birds have a band,
With a squirrel on tambourine, just as planned.
The thrush croons a ballad, so sweet and so bright,
While the owls read the lyrics out loud in the night.

"Who's on the flute?" asks a wise old crow,
"Not me!" says the thrush, "I'm just here for the show!"
A juggler of apples appears out of air,
"Watch me!" he calls, "It's a fruity affair!"

The breezes are clapping; you can hear the trees chuckle,
As the blossoms join in with a delicate rustle.
The humor of nature flows smooth as a breeze,
With melodies carefree, like jazz in the leaves.

And when the night falls, they all share a cheer,
Nature's own concert, always drawing us near.
So join in the fun, let your worries take flight,
In the harmony of foliage, everything's right!

www.ingramcontent.com/pod-product-compliance
Lightning Source LLC
Chambersburg PA
CBHW072132070526
44585CB00016B/1636